PAT METHENY
GUITAR ETUDES

ISBN 978-1-4584-1173-0

HAL•LEONARD®
CORPORATION
7777 W. BLUEMOUND RD. P.O. BOX 13819 MILWAUKEE, WI 53213

Visit Hal Leonard Online at
www.halleonard.com

INTRODUCTION

One of the most common questions I am asked by students is, "What kinds of things do you do to warm up before a concert?" Over the years, in many master classes and workshops around the world, I have demonstrated the kind of daily workout I put myself through, and there has always been a lot of interest in the process. This book is a first attempt to address this area in a more detailed way.

To me, warming up is an essential part of every performance. Before every concert, I need to spend at least an hour with the instrument in hand, getting loose with it. However, since my main focus is improvisation, I have always searched for a way to combine a physical workout with the spontaneous creation of harmonic and melodic material. This prepares my mind for what improvisation involves without actually "practicing" improvisations on a specific tune or form. What I wind up doing is different every time.

These etudes are my actual transcriptions from a week of warm-ups during a concert tour in Italy in the summer of 2010. Basically, I placed a small recording device in front of me and just did what I always do. These pieces are all improvised, but they are functional on a guitaristic level. They get one moving all over the instrument, and hopefully, also provide a certain musical satisfaction.

Essentially, my method is to take ideas that I don't really have to think about too much, move them through keys, and just sort of let them spin out. I do my best to follow things to what seems to be either a natural conclusion, or to make a link to the next idea and follow that, and so on. To me, these pieces follow the idea of "automatic writing," in that they just unfold.

In essence, it is exactly the same set of priorities that I follow when actually improvising in concert, but with a different set of aesthetic values. The ideal result of all of this would be to walk out on stage warmed-up, prepared, and ready to go without ever having "thought" of any particular idea, so that the first solo of the first tune is really the first moment of the day that I am fully engaged in the more narrative type of playing that I aspire to.

Hopefully these transcriptions will accomplish two things; I think they provide a good workout (encouraging movement all over the instrument), but I also hope that they offer some ideas about how to generate your own set of materials for a complete warm-up, without having to play the same thing every time.

–Pat Metheny

Exercise 1
(Borgia)
by Pat Metheny

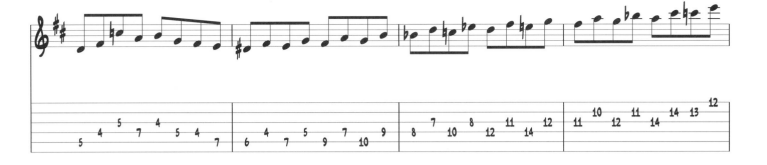

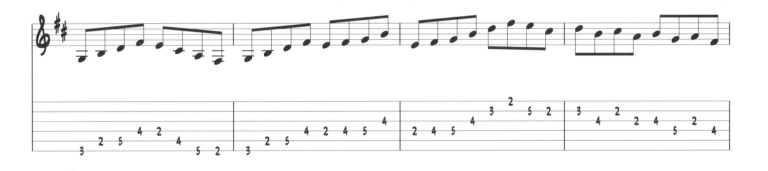

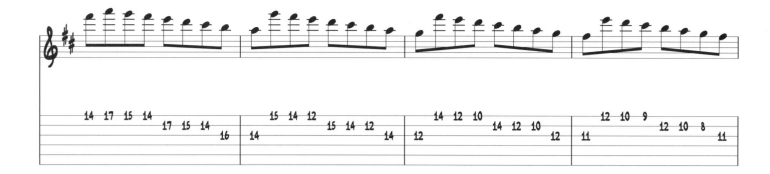

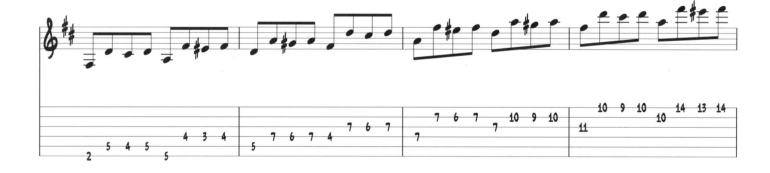

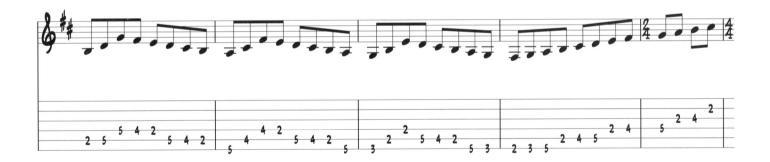

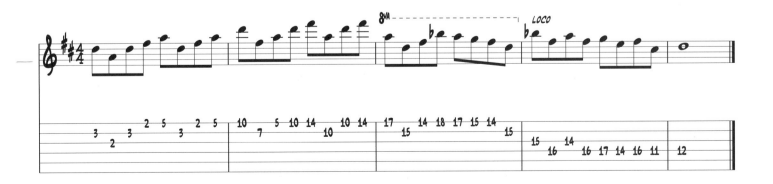

Exercise 2
(Borgia)

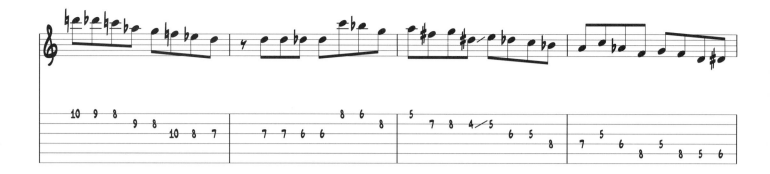

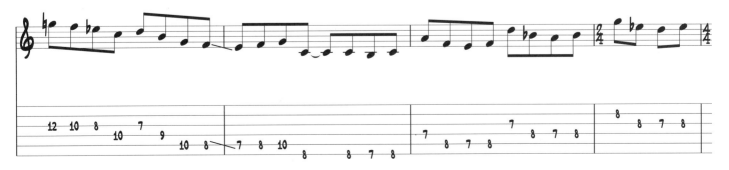

11

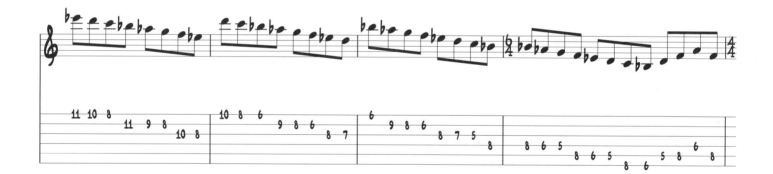

EXERCISE 3
(BORGIA)

Exercise 4
(Borgia)

Exercise 5
(Borgia)

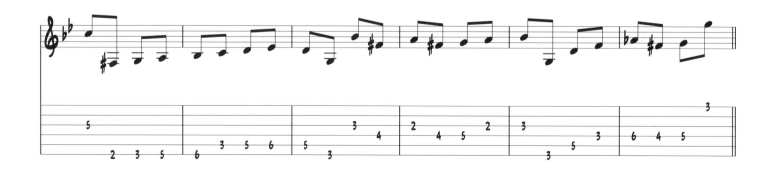

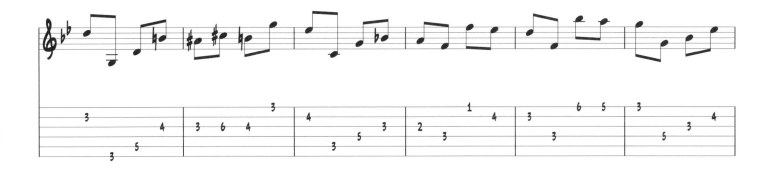

EXERCISE 6
(BORGIA)

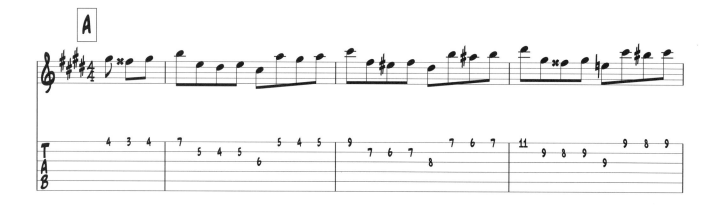

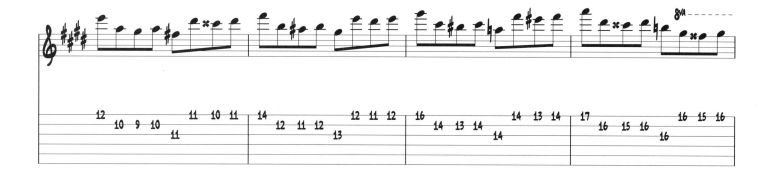

Exercise 7
(Pescara)

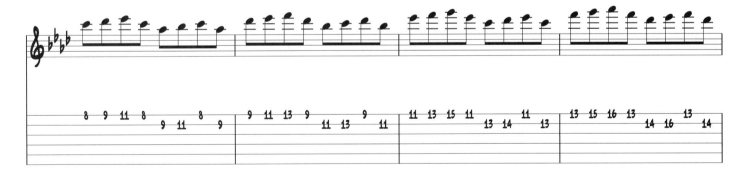

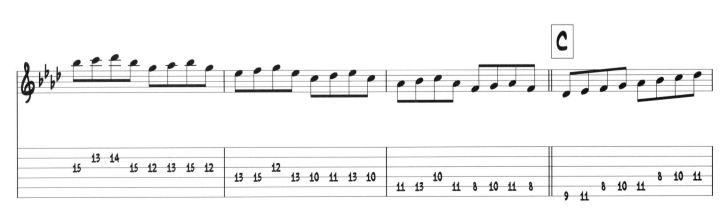

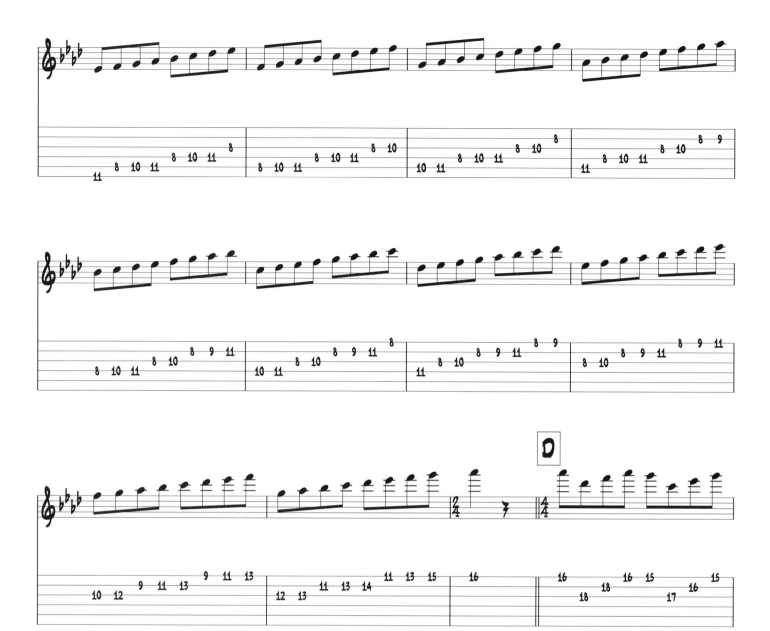

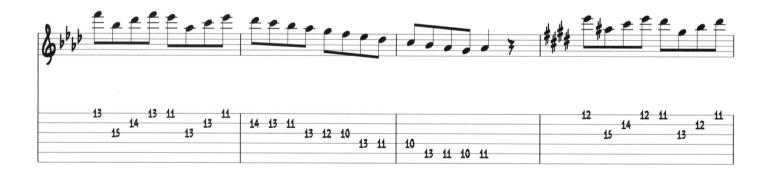

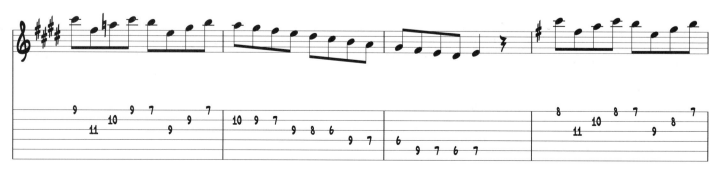

26

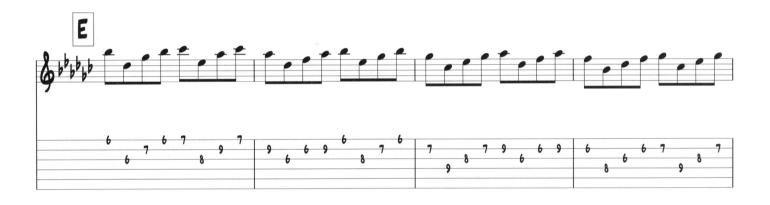

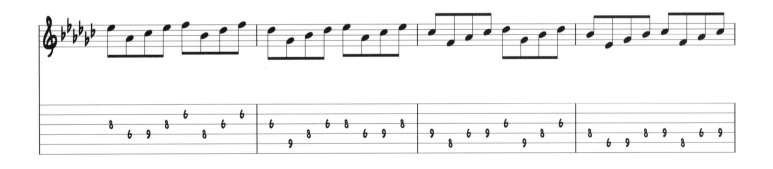

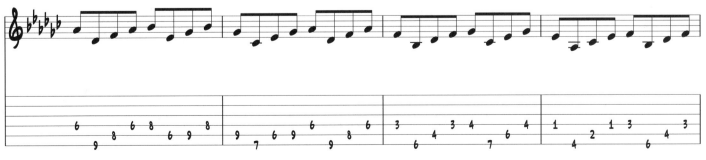

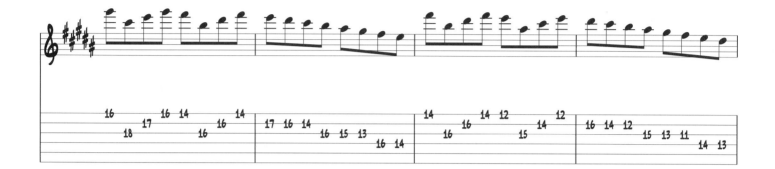

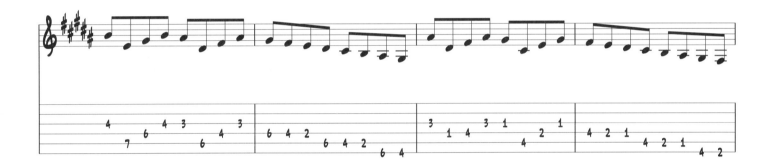

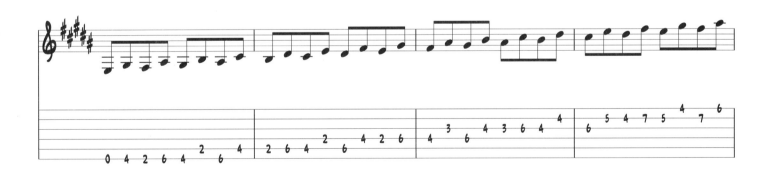

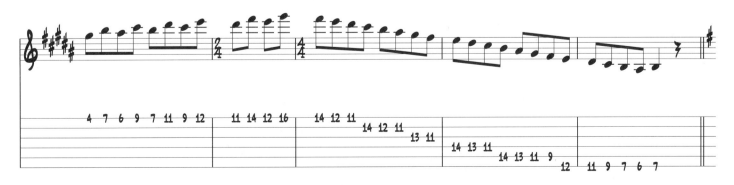

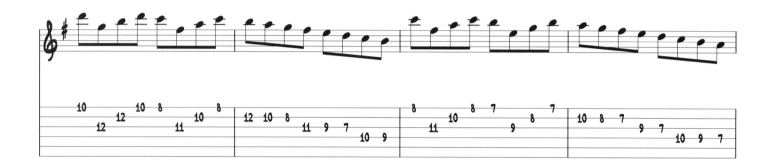

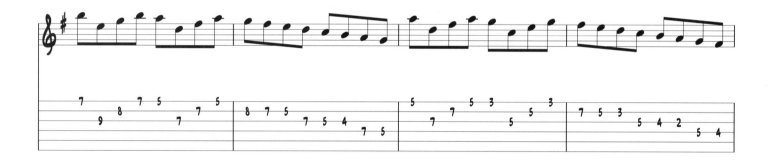

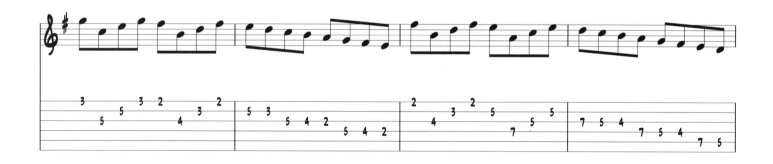

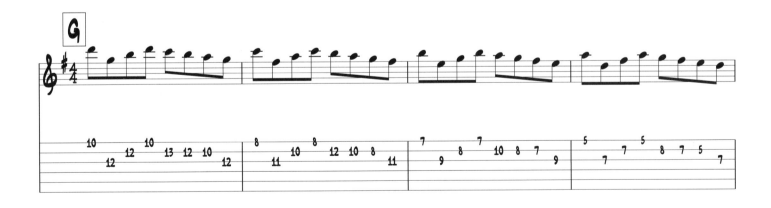

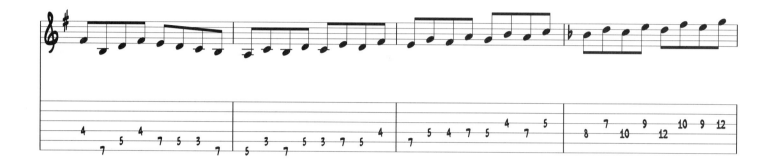

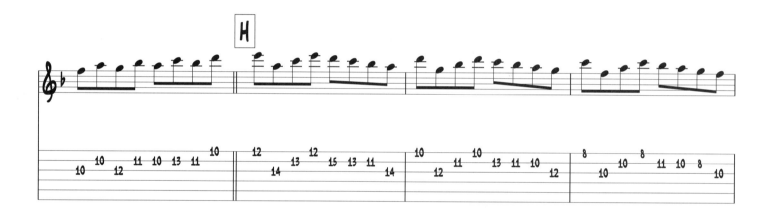

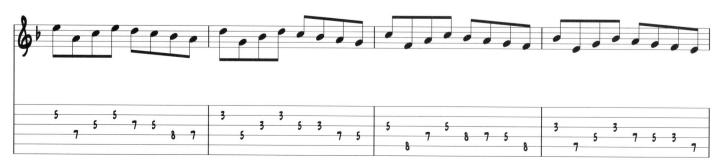

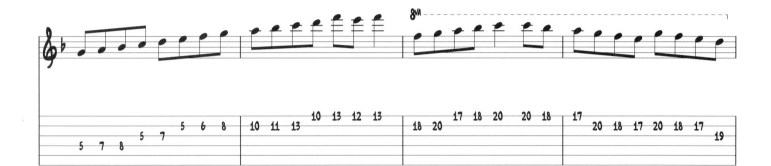

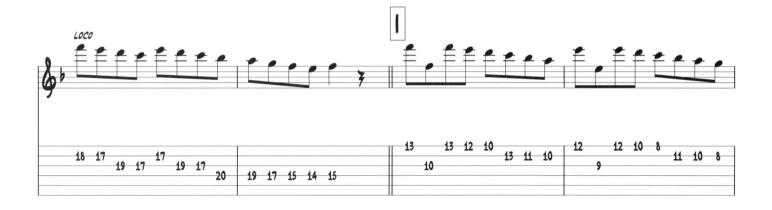

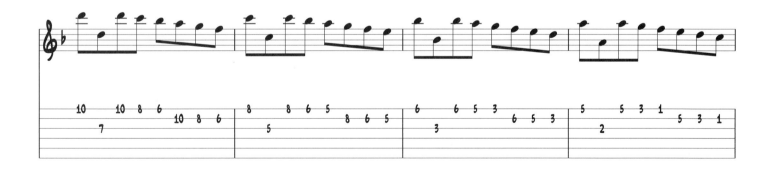

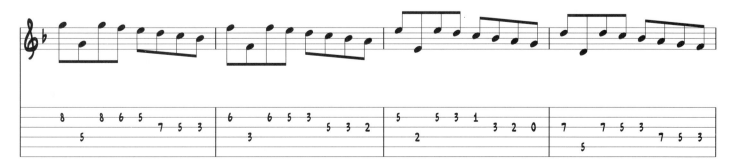

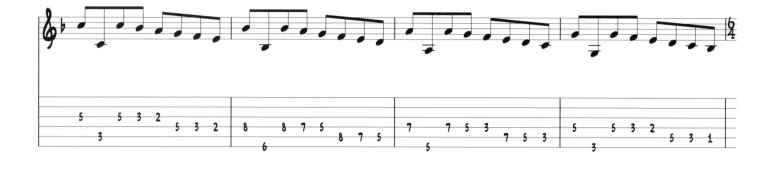

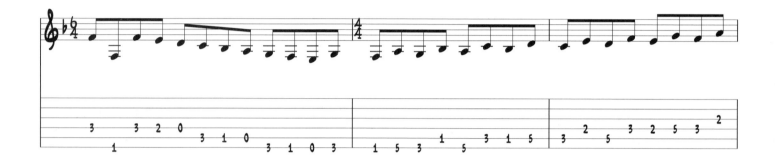

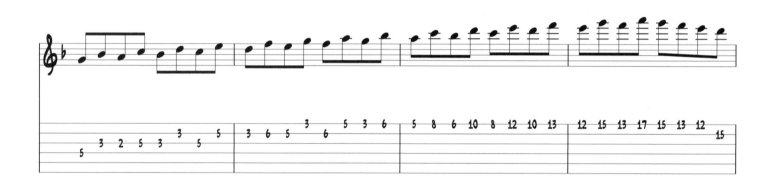

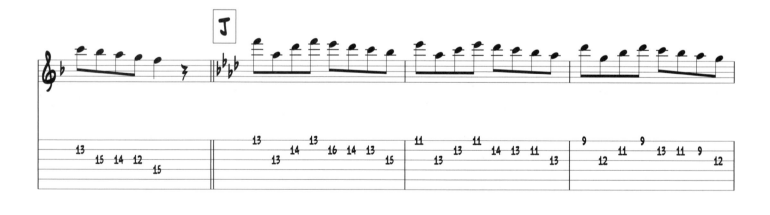

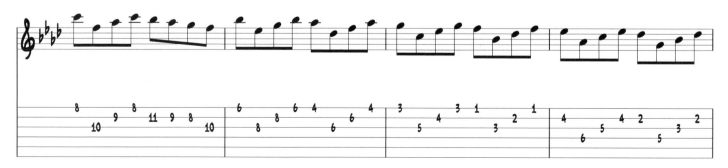

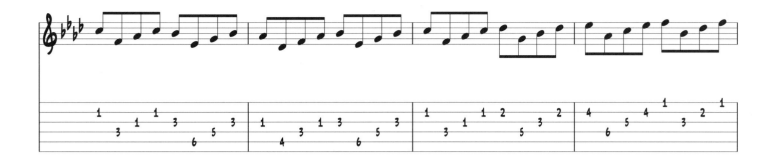

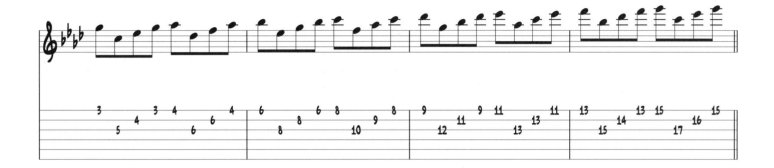

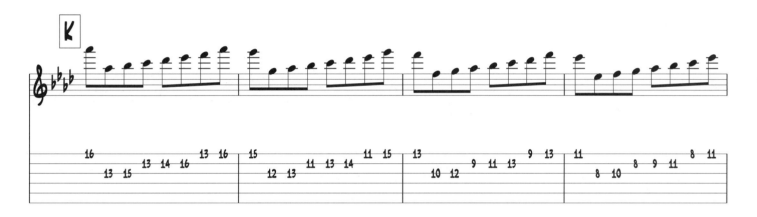

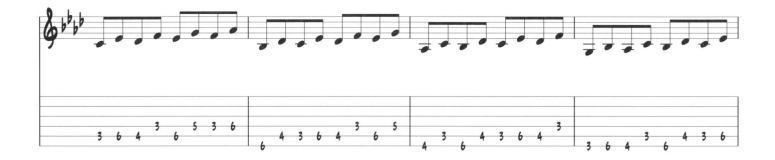

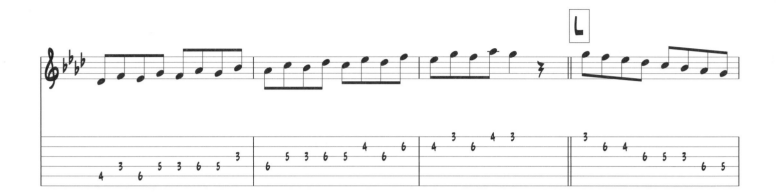

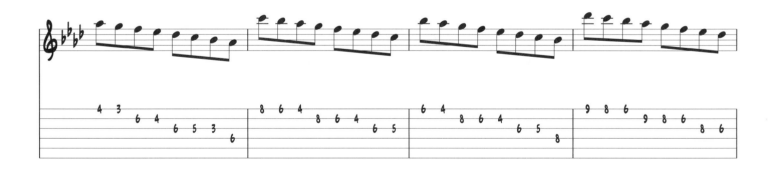

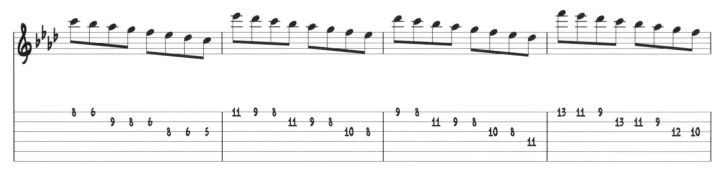

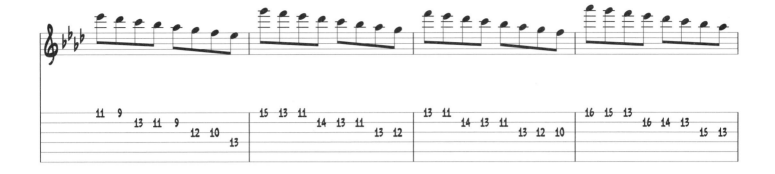

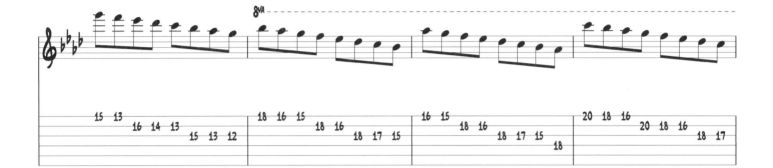

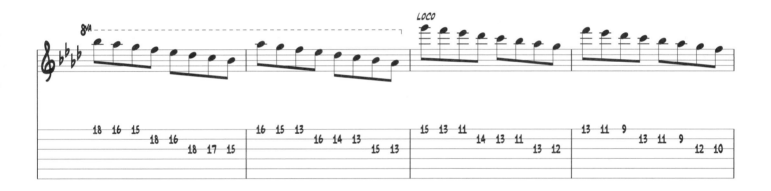

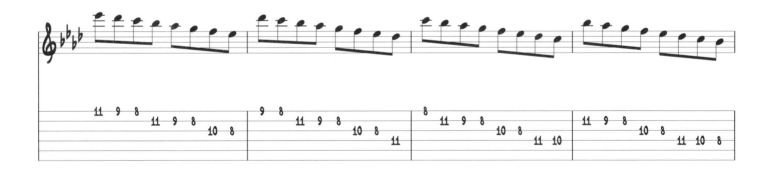

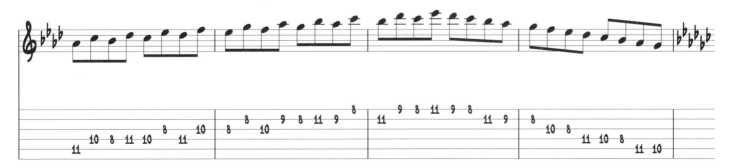

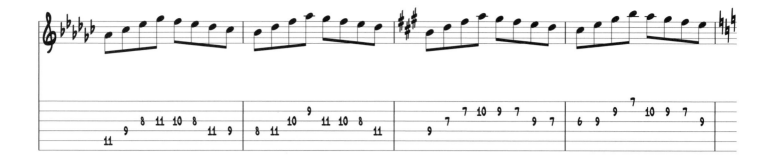

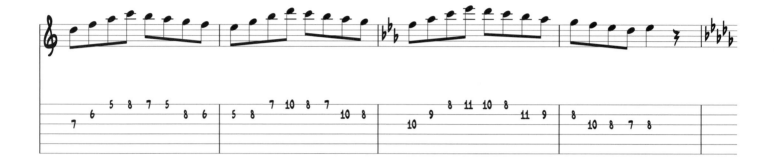

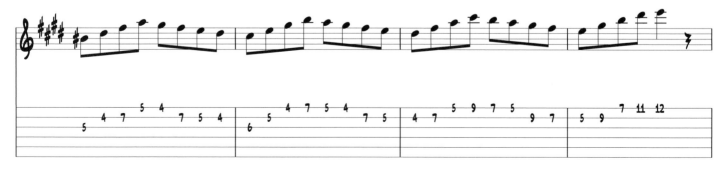

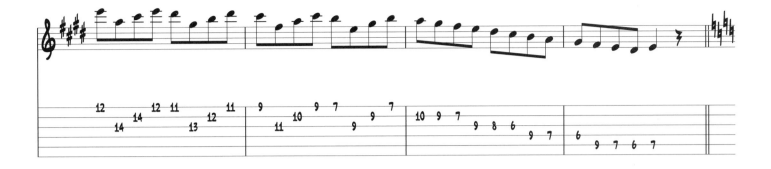

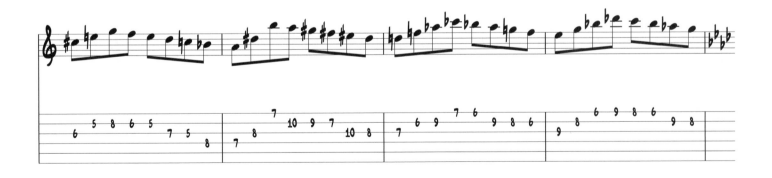

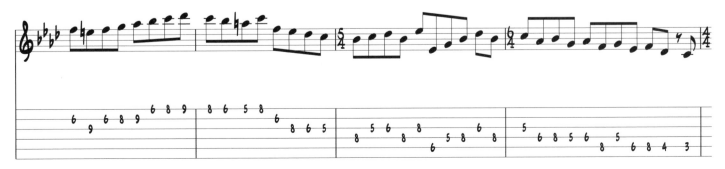

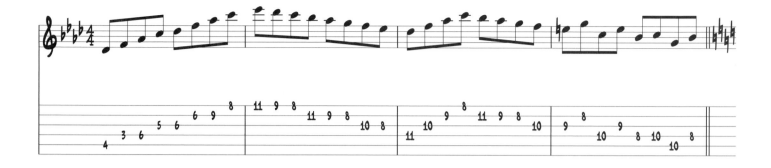

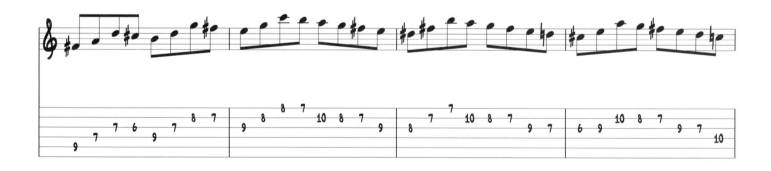

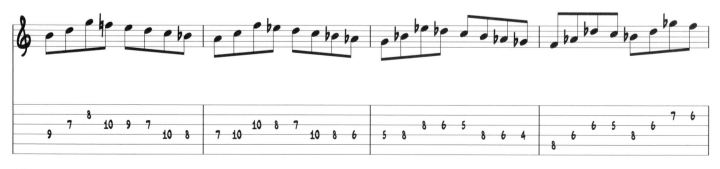

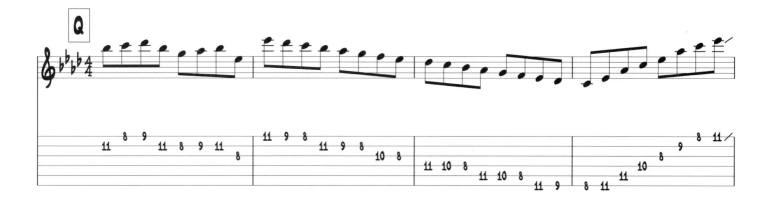

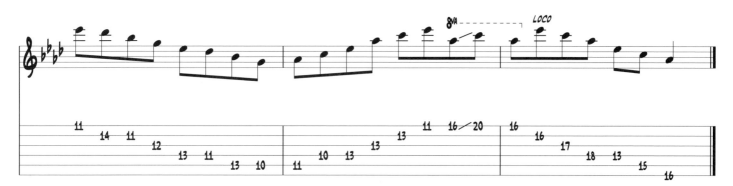

Exercise 8
(Pescara)

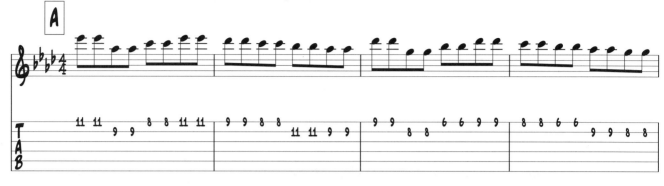

42

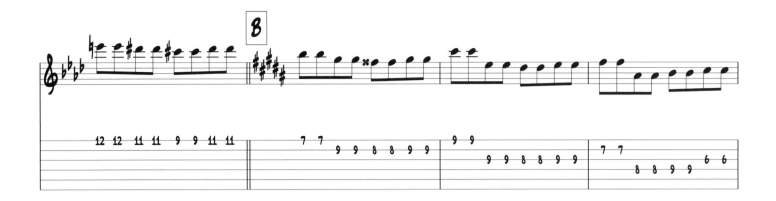

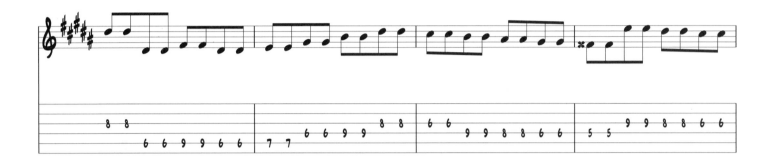

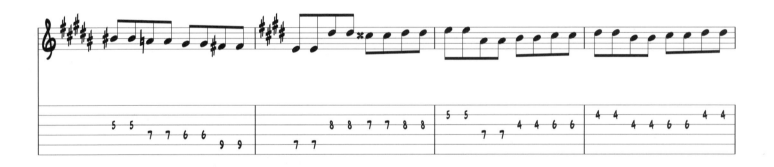

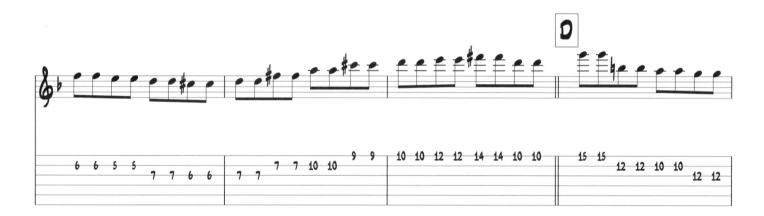

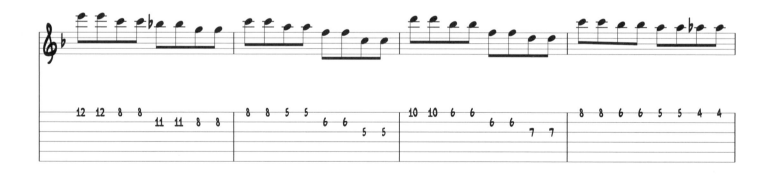

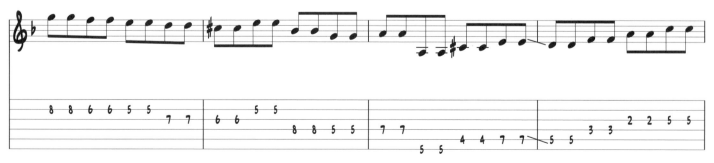

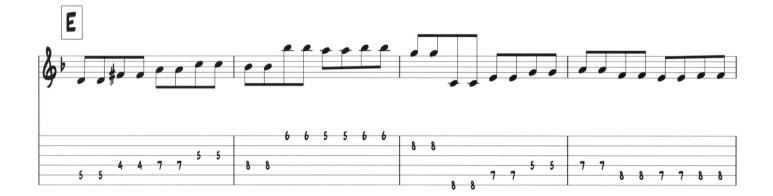

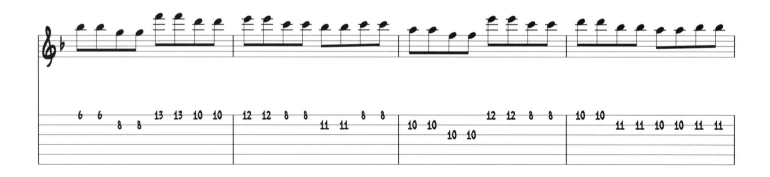

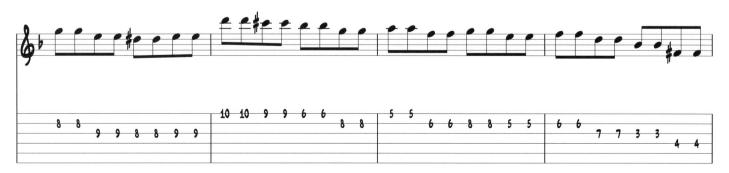

F

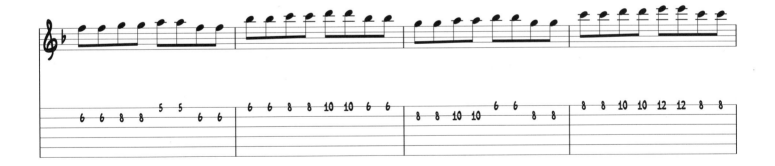

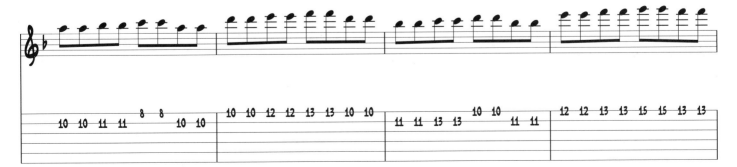

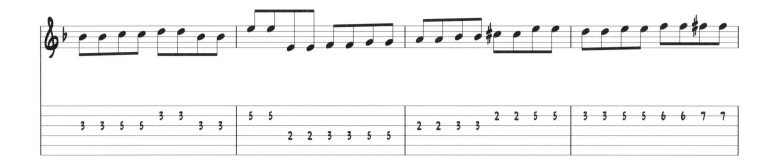

H

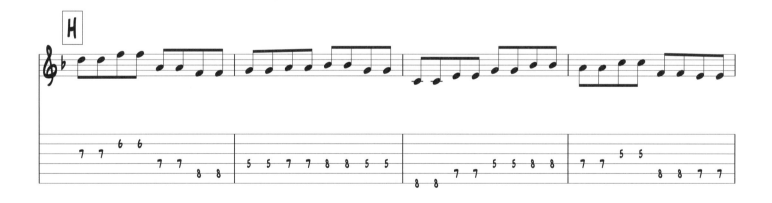

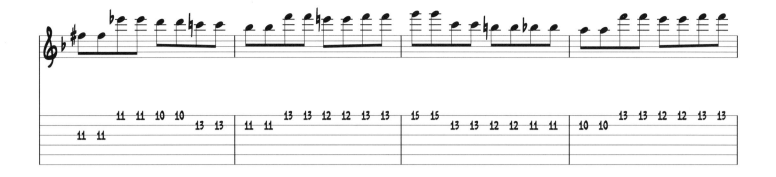

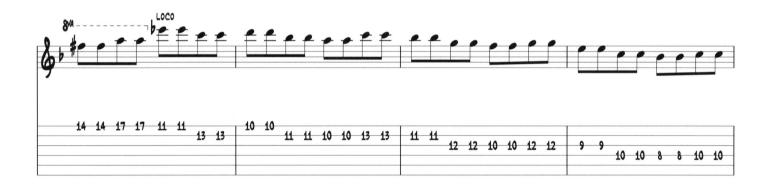

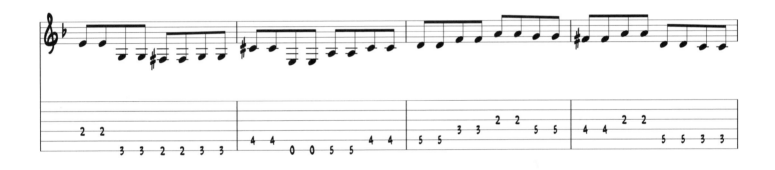

Exercise 9
(Pescara)

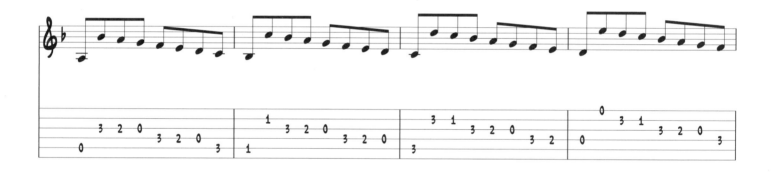

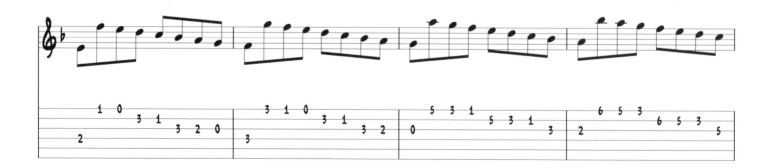

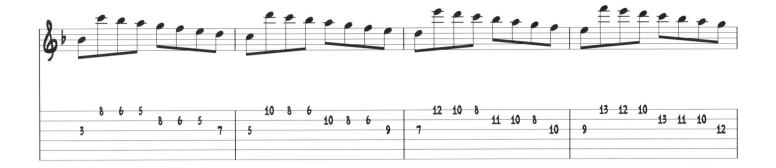

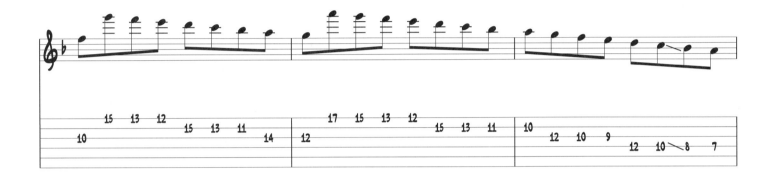

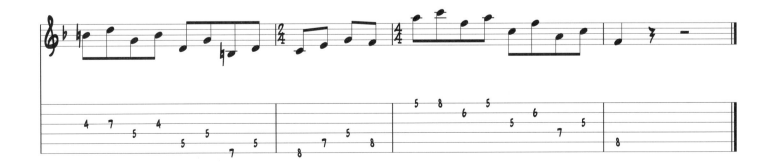

Exercise 10
(Pescara)

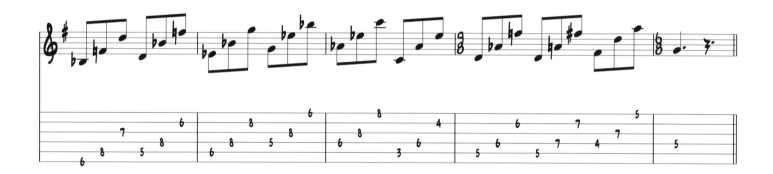

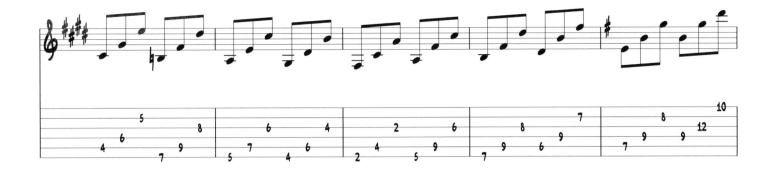

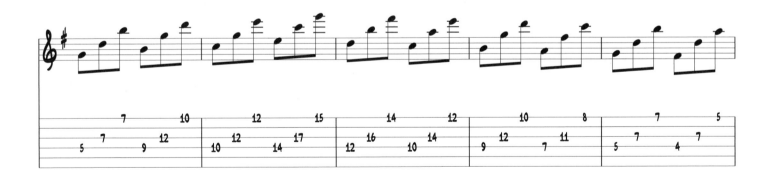

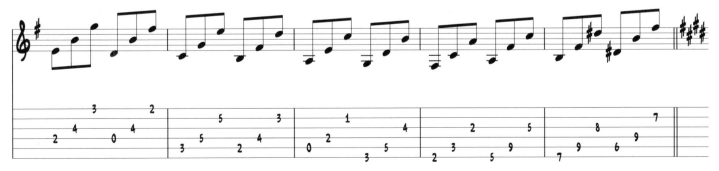

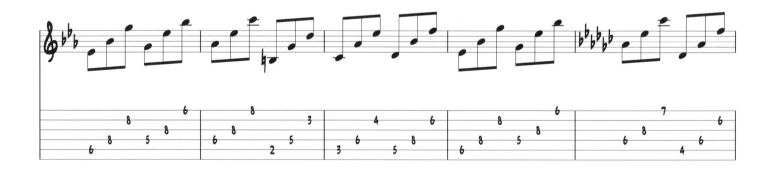

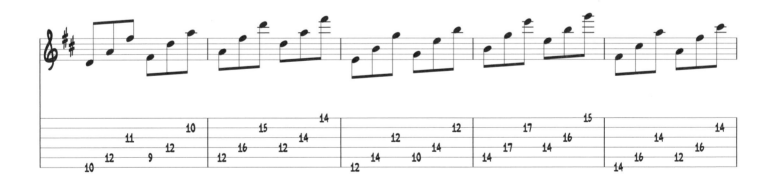

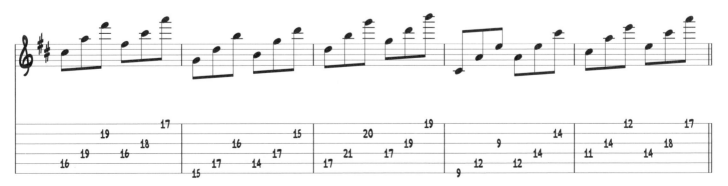

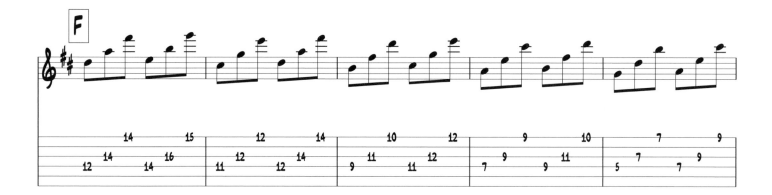

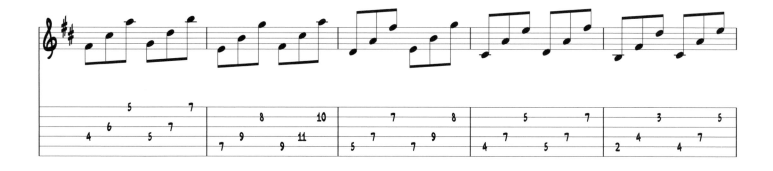

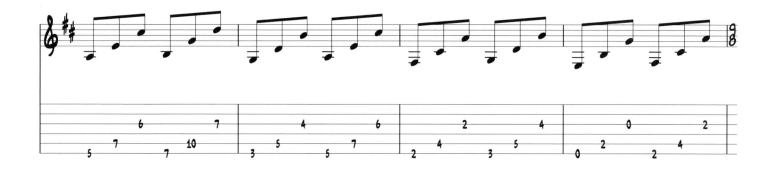

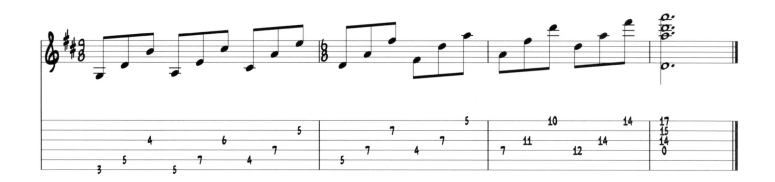

EXERCISE 11
(PESCARA)

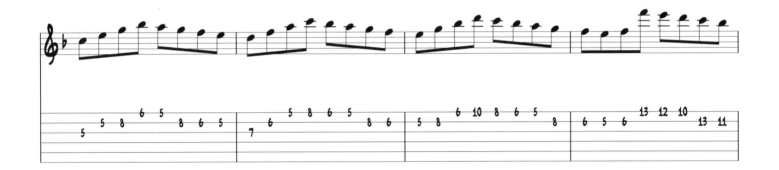

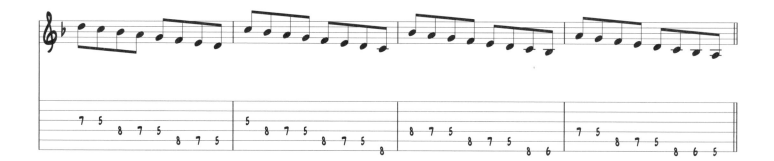

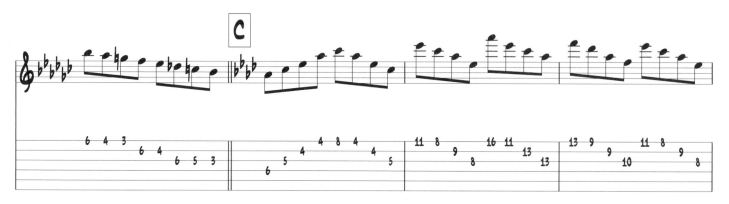

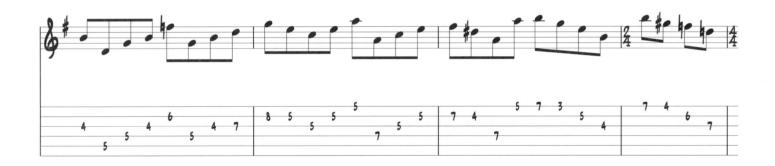

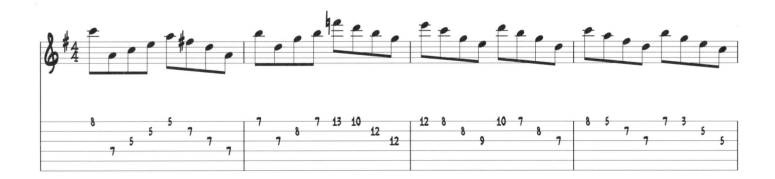

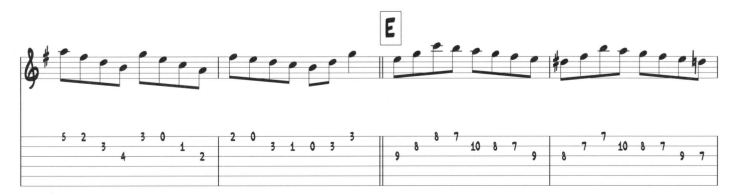

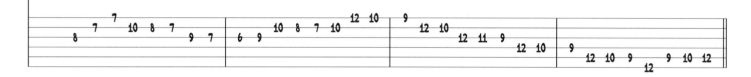

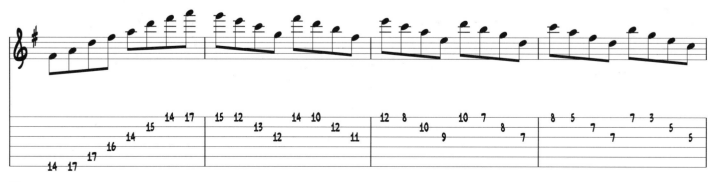

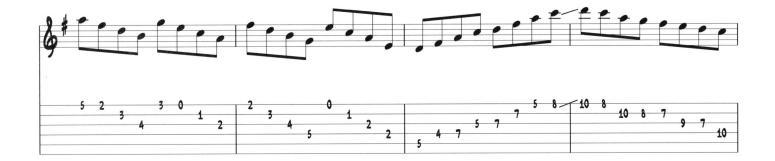

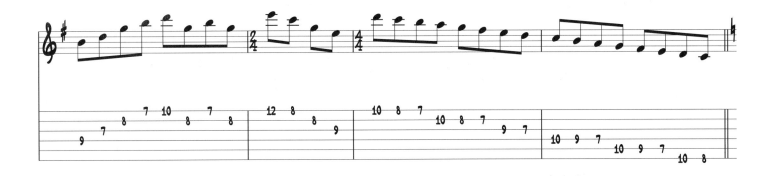

EXERCISE 12
(PERUGIA)

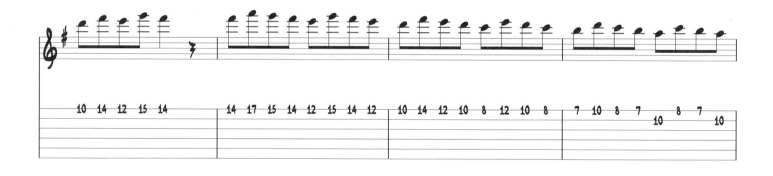

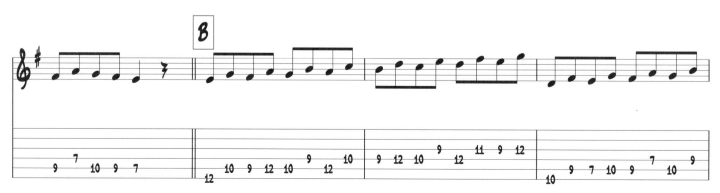

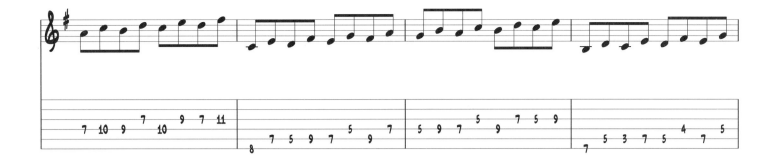

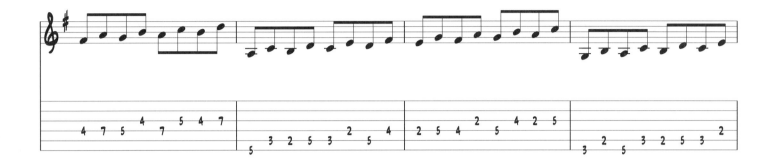

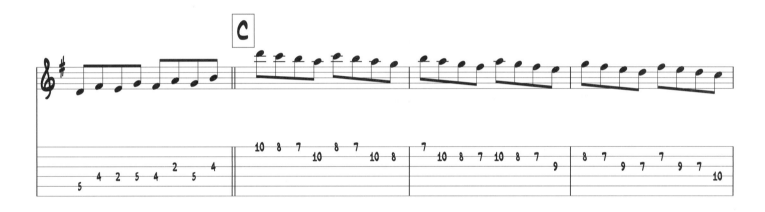

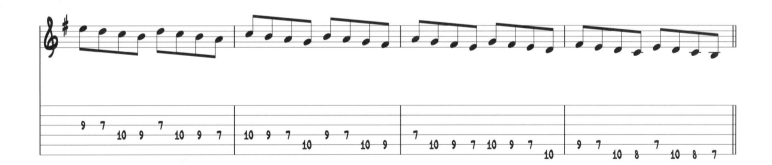

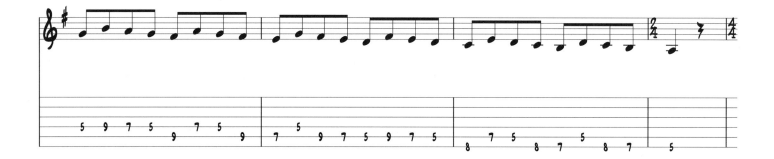

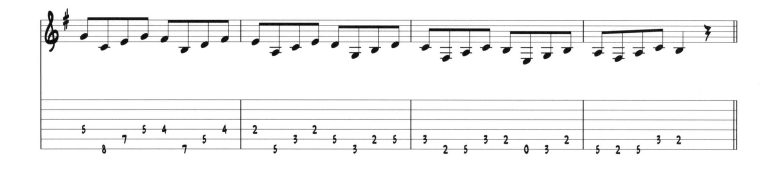

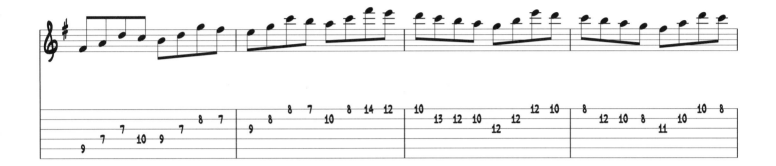

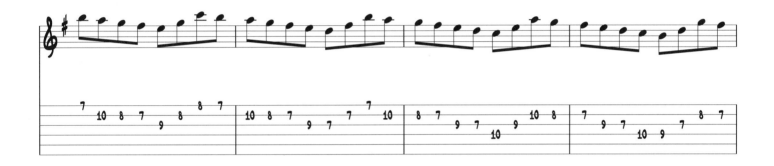

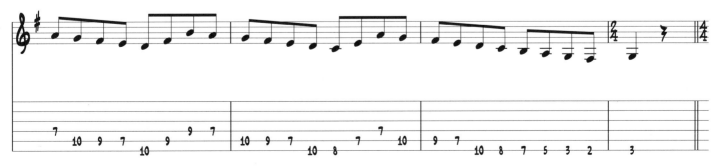

G

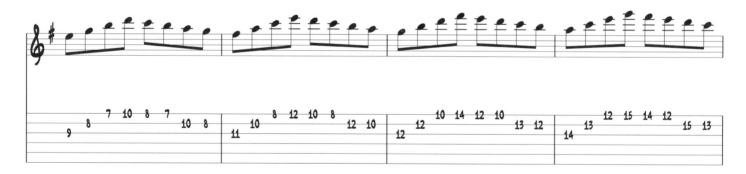

H

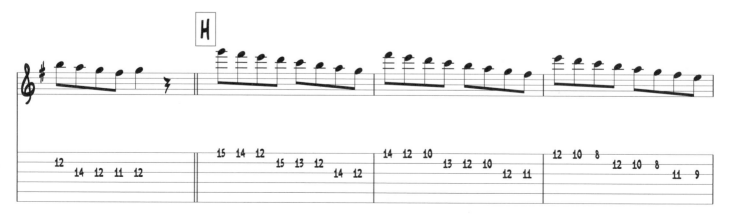

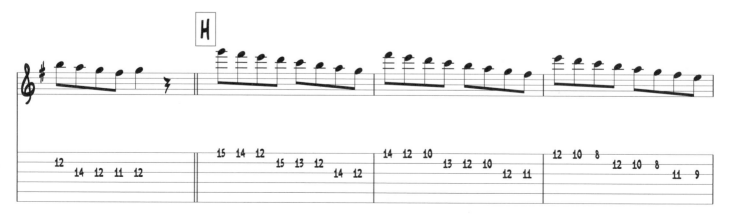

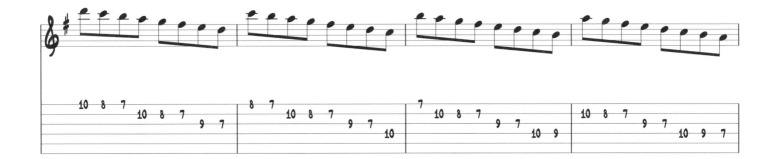

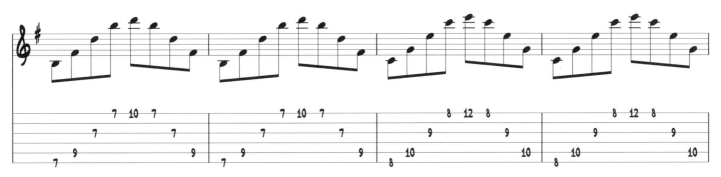

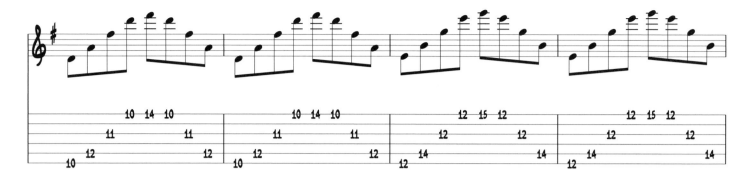

J

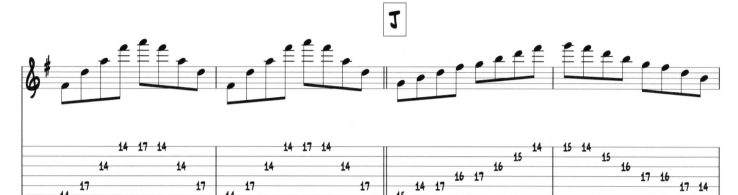

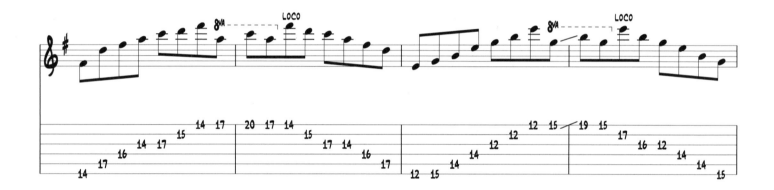

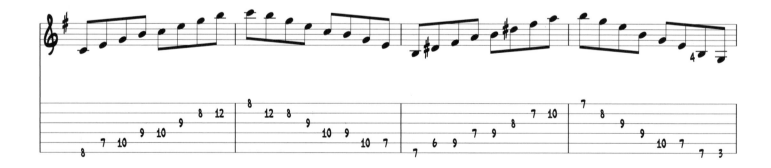

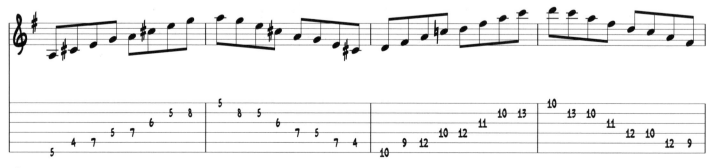

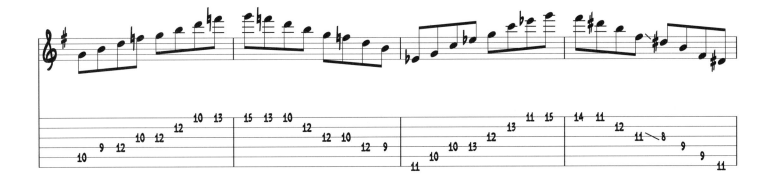

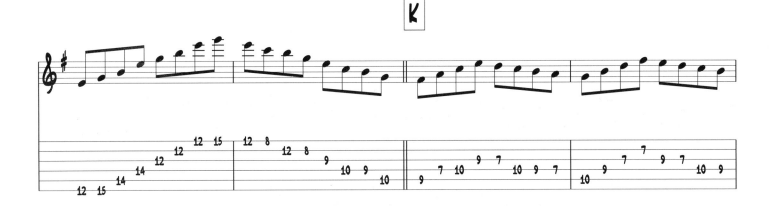

K

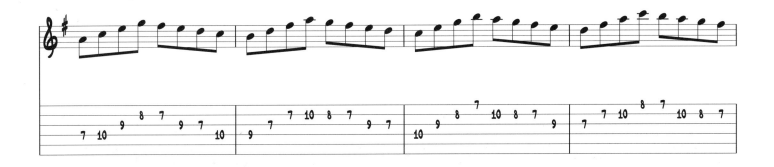

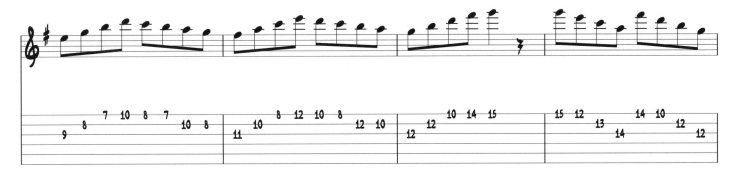

L

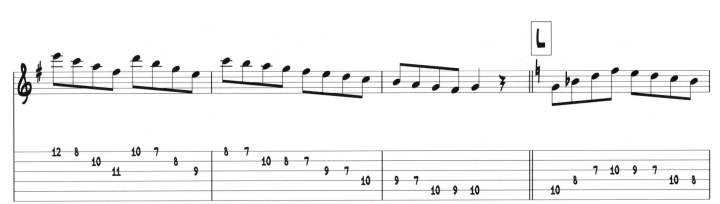

71

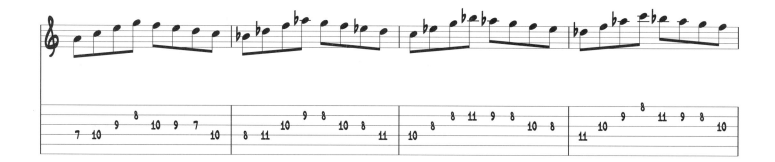

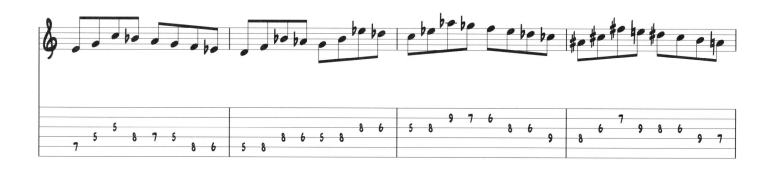

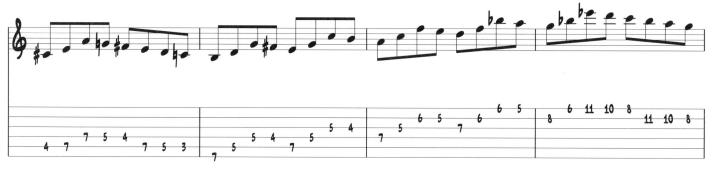

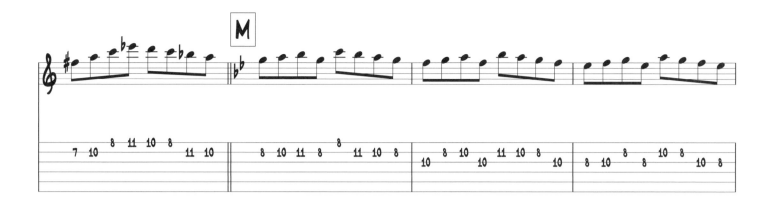

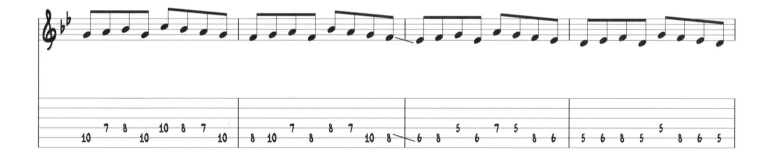

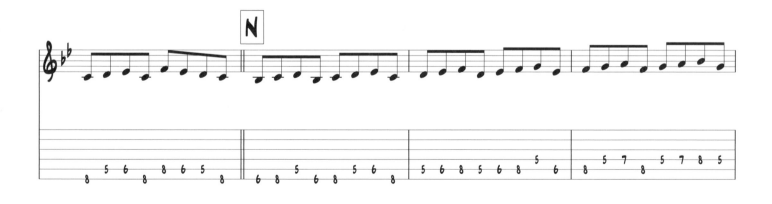

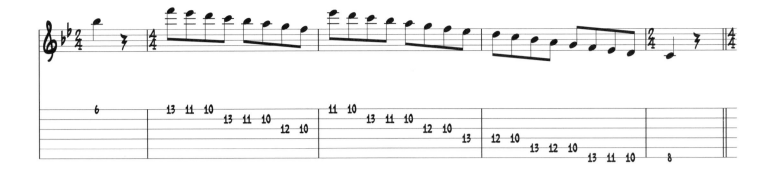

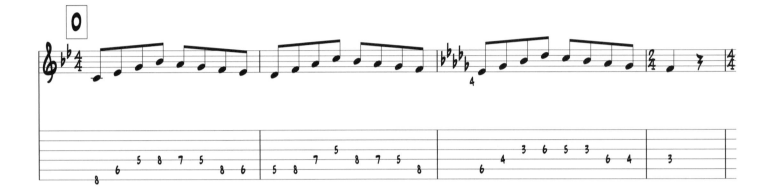

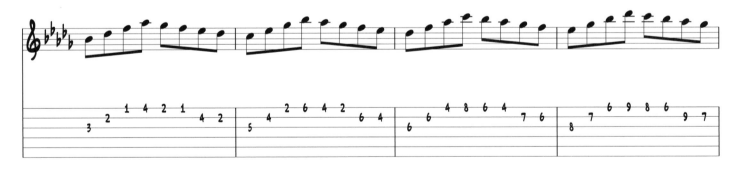

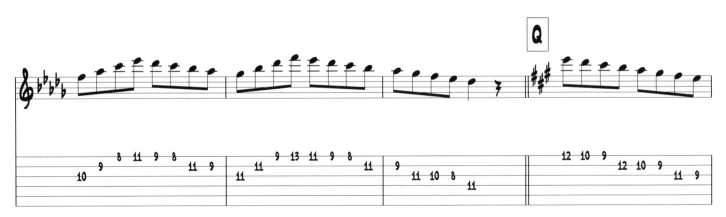

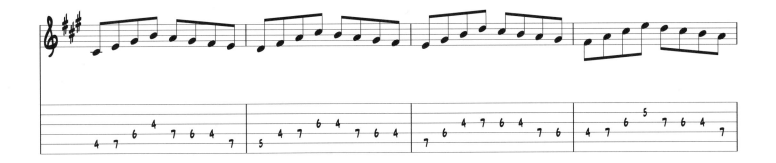

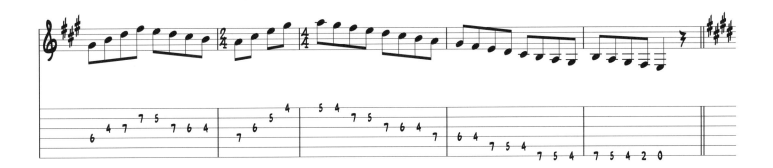

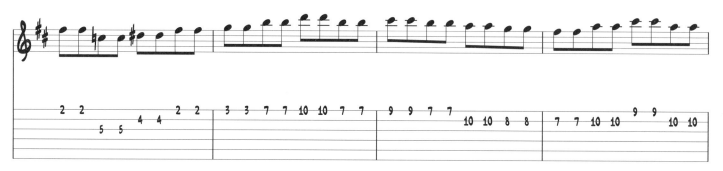

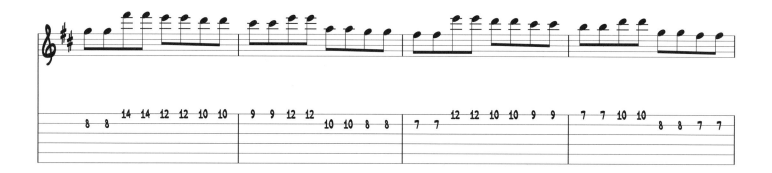

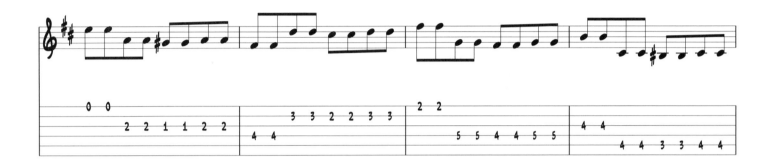

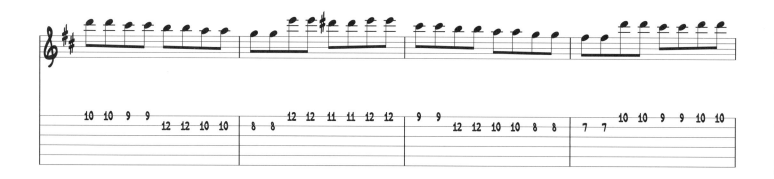

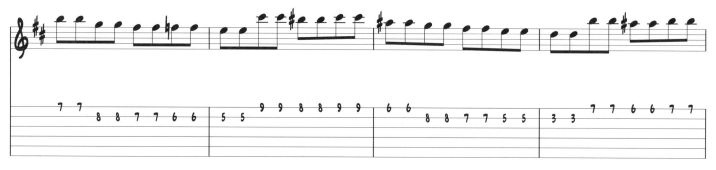

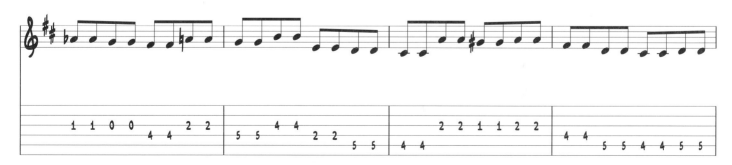

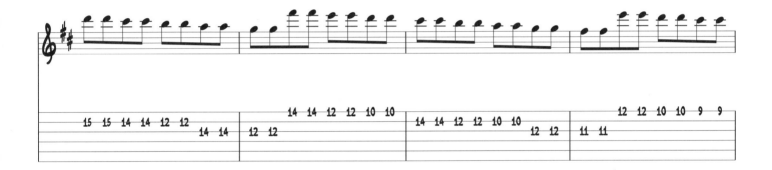

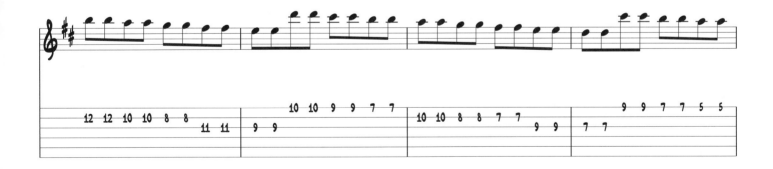

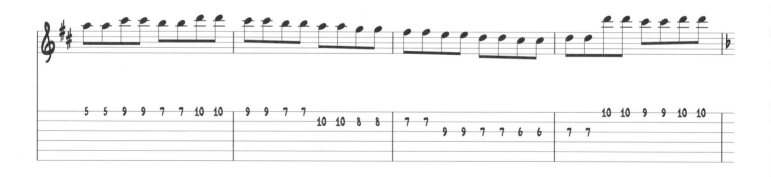

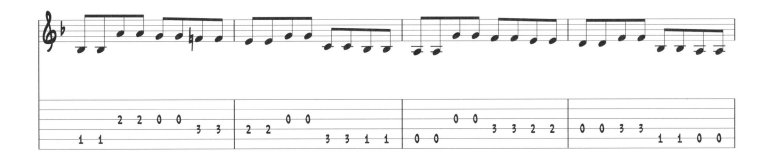

Exercise 13
(Aosta)

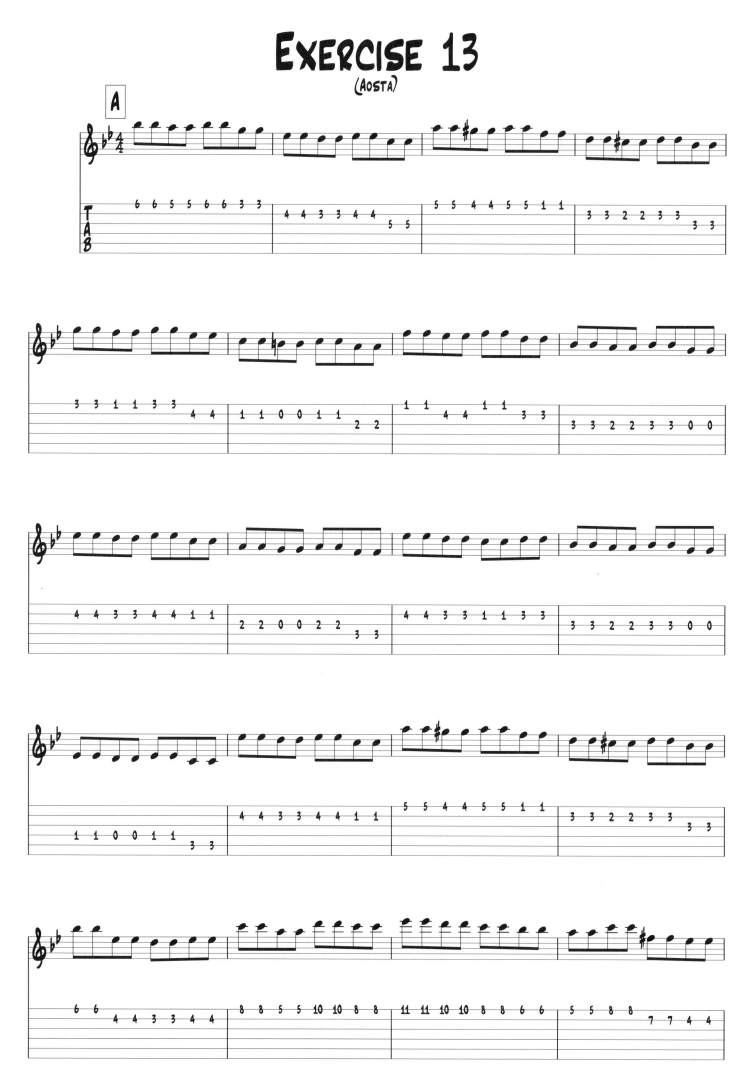

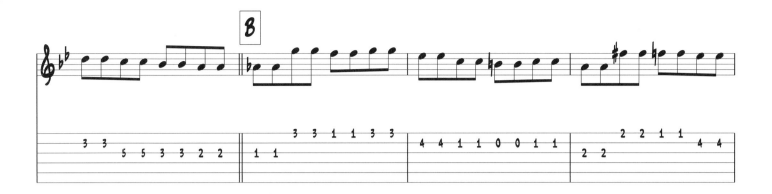

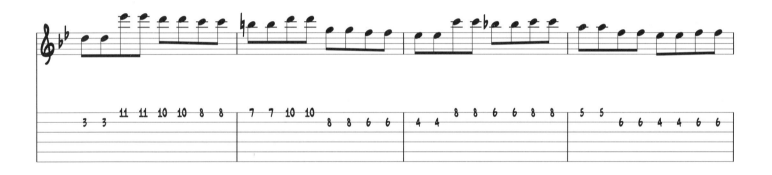

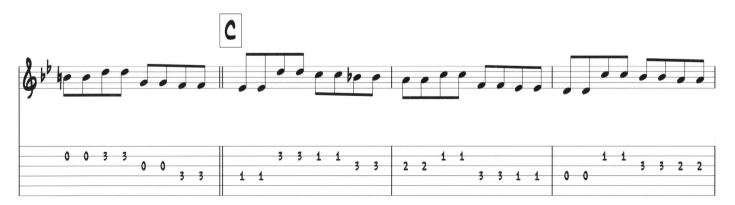

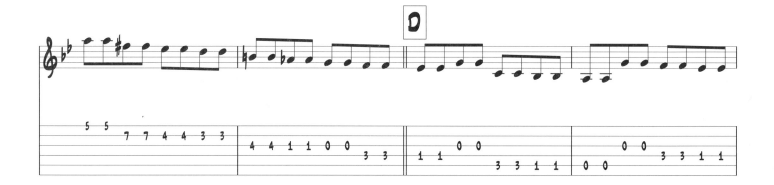

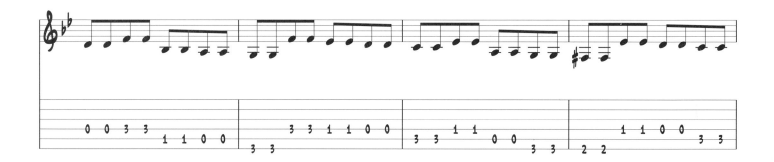

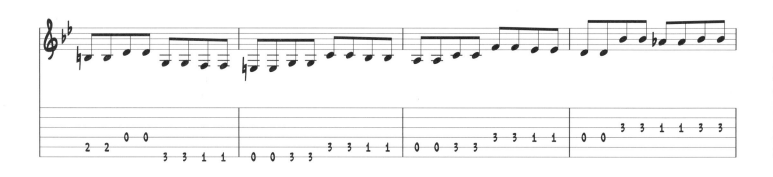

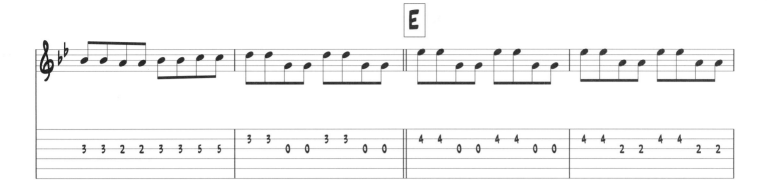

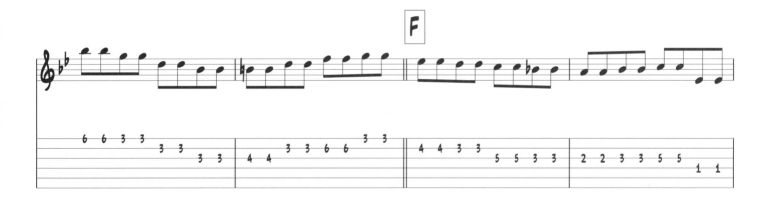

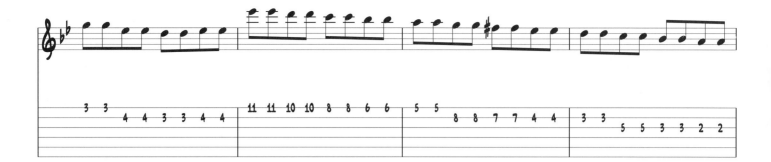

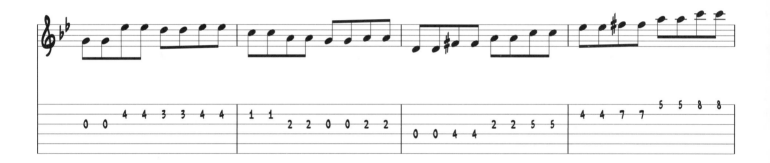

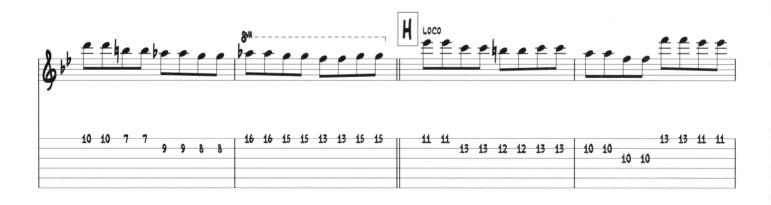

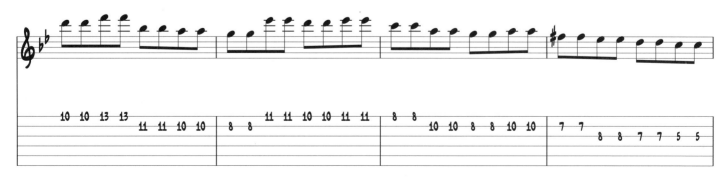

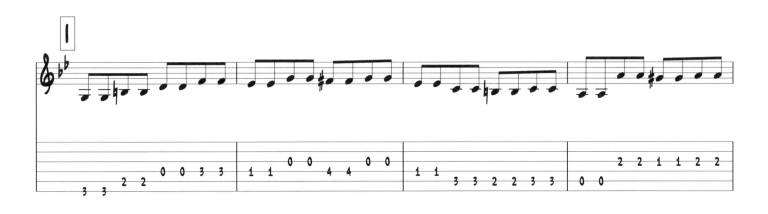

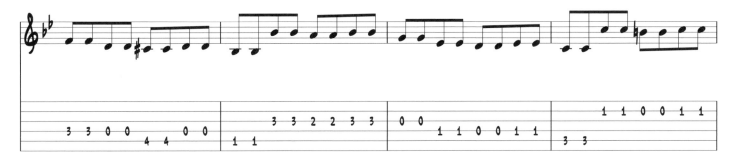

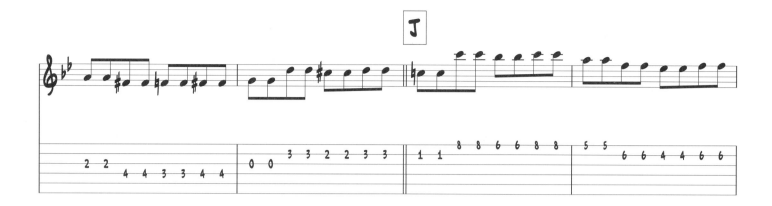

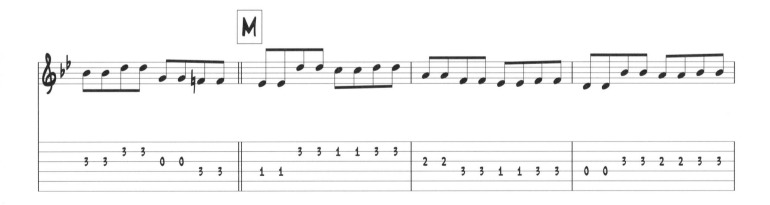

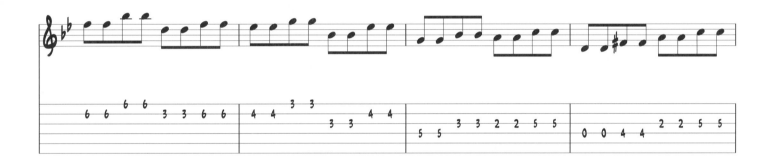

Exercise 14
(Venice)

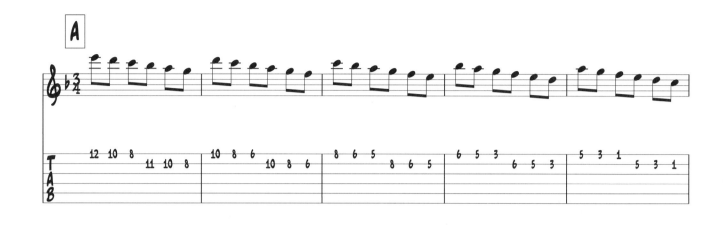

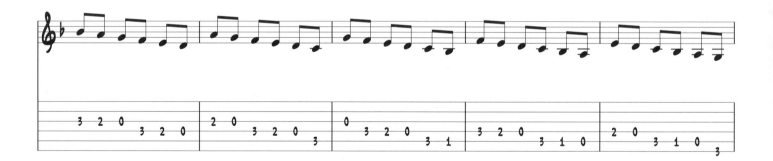

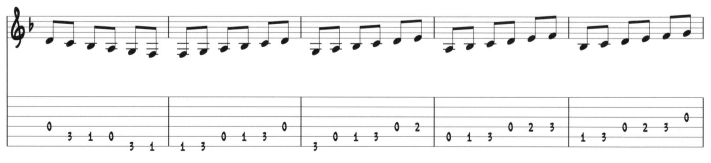

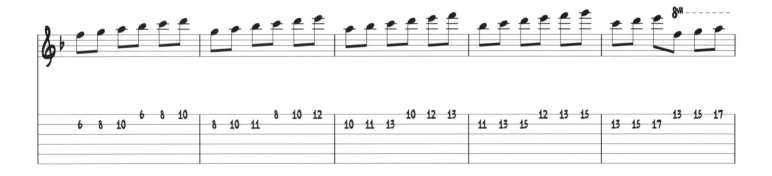

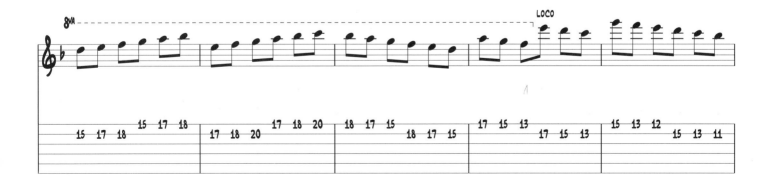

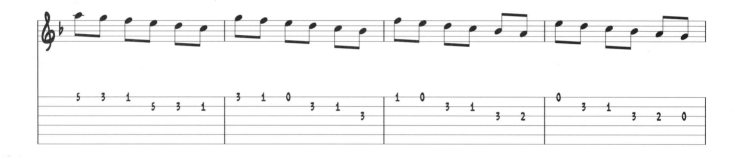

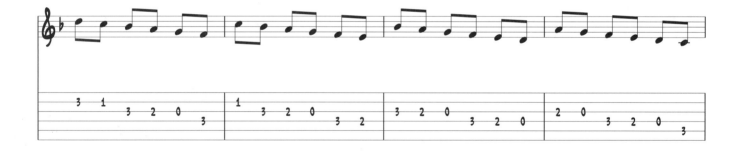